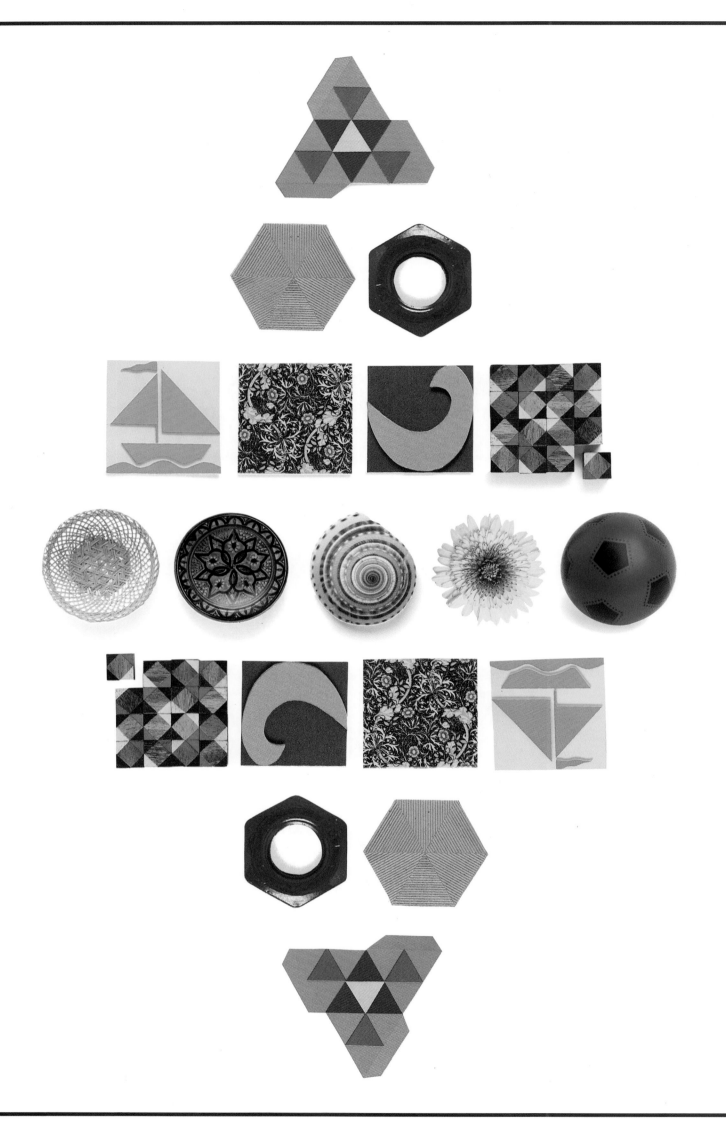

The Amazing Book of Shapes

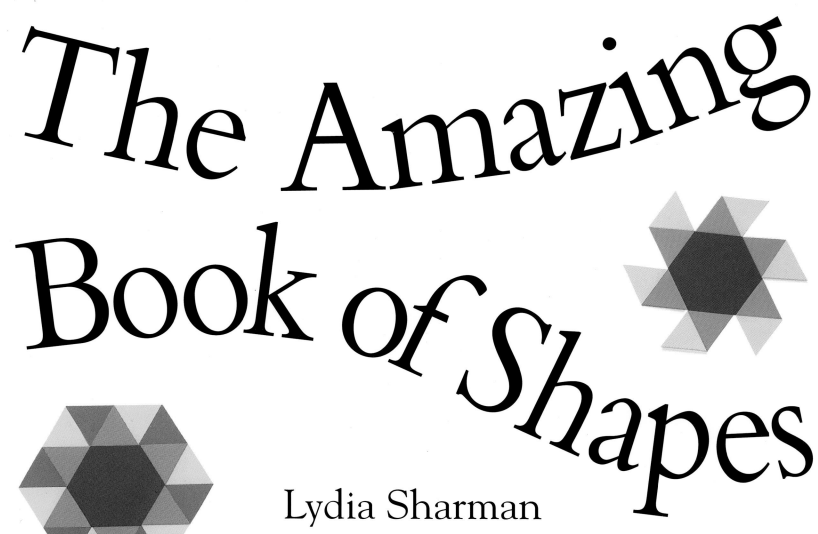

Lydia Sharman

Scholastic Canada Ltd.

A Dorling Kindersley Book

For Julia and Sarah Ferrabee

Project editor   Monica Byles
U.S. editor   B. Alison Weir
Art editor   Jane Horne

Managing editor   Jane Yorke
Managing art editor   Chris Scollen
Production   Shelagh Gibson
Picture research   Christine Rista
Photography   Steve Gorton
Illustrations   Janos Marffy, Grahame Corbett

First published in Great Britain in 1994 by
Dorling Kindersley Limited
9 Henrietta Street, London WC2E 8PS

Published in Canada in 1994 by
Scholastic Canada Ltd.
123 Newkirk Road, Richmond Hill
Ontario L4C 3G5

Canadian Cataloguing in Publication Data

Sharman, Lydia
        The amazing book of shapes

ISBN   0-590-24306-3

1. Geometry – Juvenile literature.   2. Creative
activities and seat work.   I. Title.

QA445.5.S53 1994   j516'.15   C94–930308–9

Reproduced by Bright Arts
Printed and bound in Singapore by Tien Wah Press (PTE.) Ltd

Contents

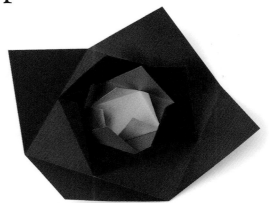

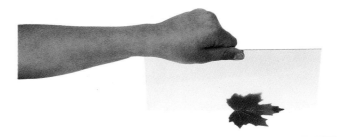

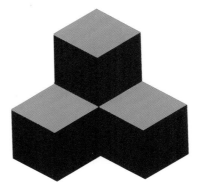

Note to parents and teachers

The **Amazing Book of Shapes** is packed with creative projects to help children absorb basic mathematical concepts of shape and pattern. Each new concept is supported by an exciting craft activity, clearly explained through step-by-step instructions and color photographs of familiar images. Take the opportunity to work through the projects in this book with your children and encourage them, whenever possible, to undertake activities in groups.

How to use this book

Encourage children to work through the early pages of this book before advancing to later projects. Once children have developed a basic understanding of shapes and patterns, they will feel confident in tackling more complex concepts.

Things you will need

All the activities in this book are based on readily available art materials. Children will need colored pencils and felt pens, white and colored paper, tracing paper, cardboard, glue, scissors, a compass, a ruler, and some poster paint.

Step-by-step activities

Step-by-step photographs and clear instructions show exactly what to do at every stage of each activity.

Patterns around the world

Colorful pictures show how a wealth of shapes and patterns are used around the world. The examples range from traditional designs to today's computer-generated images.

Through **The Amazing Book of Shapes**, children will enjoy exploring shapes and patterns and discover that finding out is fun.

Lydia Sharman

About this book

Fold-out flap

Put a sheet of paper under the fold-out flap of this book and draw inside the shape stencils to make perfect circles, squares, and triangles. The remaining stencil is half of a hexagon. Draw around this shape once, then turn the paper and draw around the shape again, joining the two halves to make a perfect hexagon. Trace the small shape outlines to make templates for tessellating shapes.

Marks around the shape stencils

The marks indicate the midpoints along the sides of each stencil shape. In addition, the circle is marked with the 12 points of a clockface and shape symbols for drawing stars and polygons.

Square and triangular grids

The square and triangular grids at the front and back of this book can be used to draw a large variety of patterns. The more detailed grid printed in the special square or triangle area on each main grid will help you draw the simple fractal patterns shown on page 31. The circles marked on the square grid will help you draw some of the patterns shown on page 29.

Mirror bookmark

The mirror bookmark can be used to test the symmetry of objects throughout the book. When the mirror is not in use, it should be looped over the top of a page to hold it safely inside the book.

Shapes and patterns

How many shapes do you know? Shapes can be flat and two-dimensional, or solid and three-dimensional. What is the difference between a circle and a sphere, or a square and a cube? Which of these shapes has the most corners?

Sphere

Rectangle

Pyramid
A pyramid is made up of four triangles on a base.

Tetrahedron
A tetrahedron is made up of three triangles on a triangular base.

Oval

Circle

Diamond

Cuboid

Square
A square is a special rectangle where all four sides are the same length.

Heart

Crescent

Pentagon

Cylinder

Hexagon

Cone

Star

Cube

Triangle

How many triangles and stars can you find?

10

Find the shapes

Most patterns are based on an arrangement of shapes. Look at this selection of patterned and plain objects. Can you describe all of the shapes you see?

How many hexagons can you find?

Can you roll a cube?

Which shapes roll?

Try rolling some different objects. They will each roll differently, according to their shape.

How does a cone roll?

How far can you roll a hoop?

11

Shapes and centers

Does every shape have a center? Use the marks printed on the sides of the shape stencils on the flap of this book to find the center of a square, a circle, and a triangle.

Find the center
Can you follow the green path to the center of this maze?

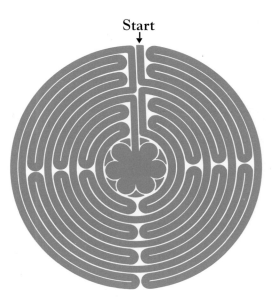

Start

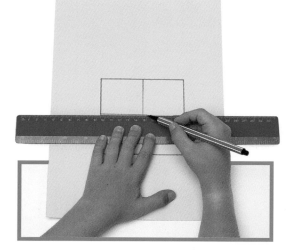

1 Draw a square using the shape stencil on the flap of this book. Mark the center point of each side.

2 Rule two lines to join the center points of the opposite sides of the square. The lines cross at the center of the square.

This maze design was built into the floor of Chartres Cathedral in France.

Centers in nature
Collect some natural objects. Does each one have a center?

Unfolding squares
Can you make these unfolding squares from four squares of paper glued one inside the other?

On their points
Alternate squares lie on their points, or on their sides.

A flower opens from its center. A snail shell grows from its center.

Take a square of paper* and fold the corners in toward the center. Now cut out a smaller square, the size of the folded square. Repeat these steps twice more.

*Turn the page to find out how to make a square from a rectangle of paper.

Using a compass

Compasses have been used for hundreds of years to draw circles. Here are some tips on how to get the best results.

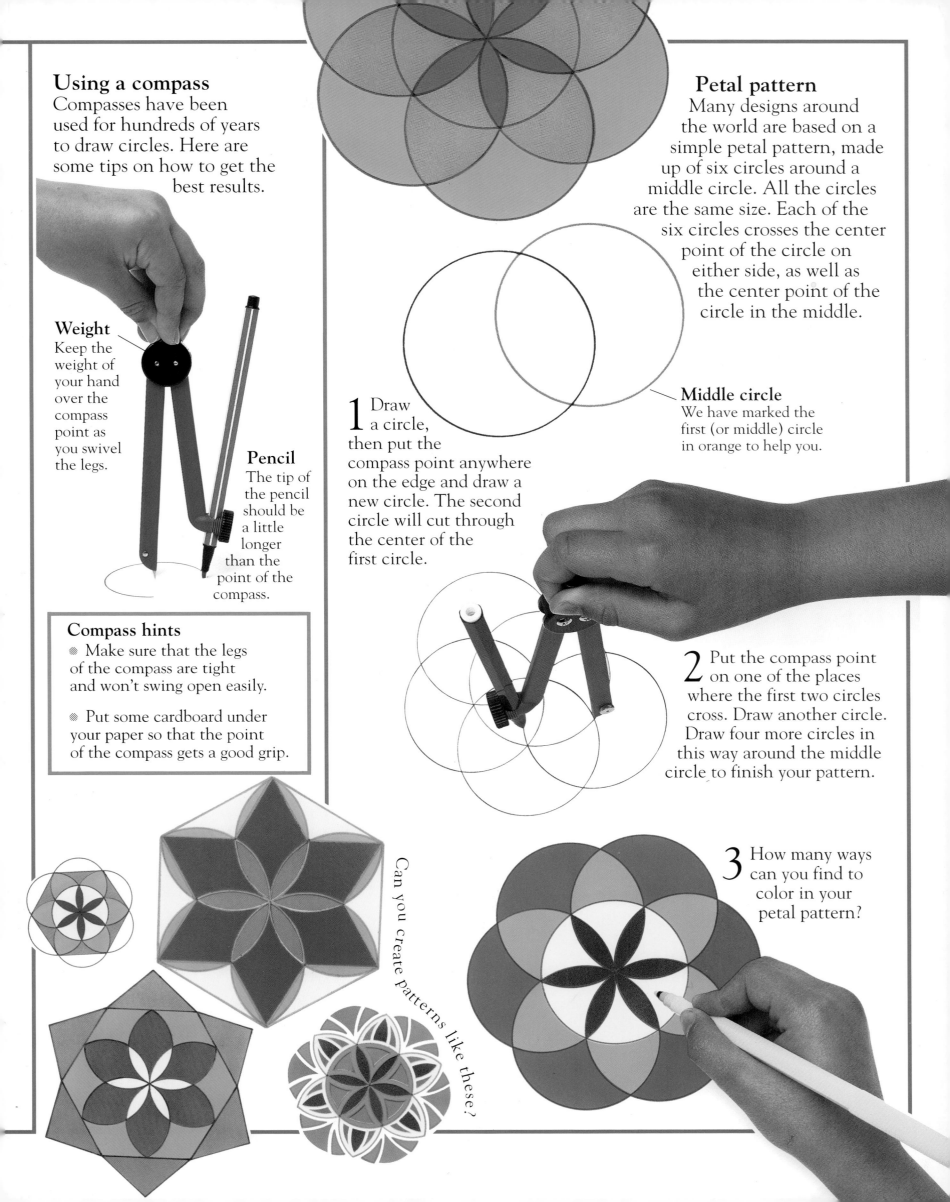

Weight
Keep the weight of your hand over the compass point as you swivel the legs.

Pencil
The tip of the pencil should be a little longer than the point of the compass.

Compass hints

❋ Make sure that the legs of the compass are tight and won't swing open easily.

❋ Put some cardboard under your paper so that the point of the compass gets a good grip.

Petal pattern

Many designs around the world are based on a simple petal pattern, made up of six circles around a middle circle. All the circles are the same size. Each of the six circles crosses the center point of the circle on either side, as well as the center point of the circle in the middle.

Middle circle
We have marked the first (or middle) circle in orange to help you.

1 Draw a circle, then put the compass point anywhere on the edge and draw a new circle. The second circle will cut through the center of the first circle.

2 Put the compass point on one of the places where the first two circles cross. Draw another circle. Draw four more circles in this way around the middle circle to finish your pattern.

3 How many ways can you find to color in your petal pattern?

Can you create patterns like these?

Parts of shapes

Can you cut different shapes into smaller parts, each of which is the same size? You can arrange these parts in different ways, but they always belong to the same whole. First try dividing a circle into equal parts. Can you figure out how to do this activity with a square and a triangle?

1 Draw a circle using the shape stencil on the flap. Now cut out the circle and fold it in half. Cut along the fold line and you have two equal halves.

2 Fold each half of the circle again and cut along each new fold line. You have made four equal parts, or quarters, from the original circle.

Equal parts
Place one part over another. What do you notice about the size and shape of the two parts?

3 Fold each quarter in half and cut along each fold again. How many parts do you have now? Can you arrange all the parts back into a circle?

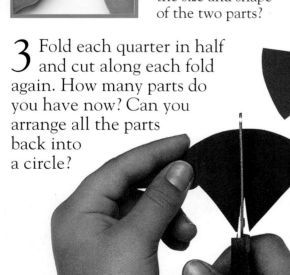

Part patterns
How many different patterns can you make with the parts?

Mystery shapes
Can you figure out which whole shapes these equal parts belong to?

Pair puzzles
Trace this pair of equal shapes onto paper and cut them out. What whole shape do they make?

Twin test
What two shapes can you make with these two equal halves?

Cube challenge
Can you make these three diamonds look like a cube?

Triangle teaser
Try fitting together these four triangles to make one large triangle.

Kirigami flowers

You can make paper flowers from a plain, square sheet of paper. Each flower you make will be different. This Japanese art is called "kirigami."

Mobile or cards
Thread some kirigami flowers together as a mobile, or use them to decorate cards.

1 Use a rectangle of paper if you don't have a square sheet. Fold over one edge of the rectangle so that it lines up with the edge next to it.

2 Now fold the rectangle part of the sheet of paper over the top of the triangle.

3 Carefully tear along the fold and put the rectangle aside. You are now left with the triangle part, which is a square of paper folded in half.

4 Fold the triangle in half to make a smaller triangle. Now fold the smaller triangle in half again.

5 Cut patterns into the triangle. Now open out your kirigami flower.

Matt or gloss
Make kirigami flowers out of matt or shiny paper in different bright colors.

Folded edges
Don't cut away all of the folded edges!

15

Symmetry

An object or pattern has mirror symmetry when both halves are the same. Where the halves meet is called a line of symmetry. An object or pattern has rotational symmetry if the object can be turned around and still looks the same. Use the mirror bookmark or a pocket mirror to test for symmetry in the objects on these pages.

Fruit feast
Is this bowl of fruit symmetrical? Use the mirror to find out.

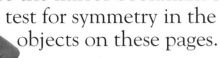

line of symmetry

Mirror symmetry
Imagine a line down the middle of an object, and lay the mirror along this line. If you can make the reflection in the mirror the same as the part hidden behind the mirror, the object has mirror symmetry. This is also called reflective symmetry.

Test the girl
This girl is not symmetrical, but if you use your mirror, you can create symmetry in the reflection.

Kaleidoscope
Put your mirror in lots of places on this colorful bag. How many symmetrical patterns can you make?

Half animals
Can you complete these pictures with your mirror to make symmetrical animals?

Fat or thin?
Can you make this spider fatter or thinner with your mirror?

Juggler
Can you make this boy juggle, or balance on two balls?

Two-headed dog?
Can you make a dog with two tails or two heads?

Two pictures in one
Can you use your mirror to find the space rocket hidden in this picture?

Rotational symmetry
If the parts of an object are the same when turned around a central point, then the object has rotational symmetry. The object will not be symmetrical when you use your mirror.

Turning box
Whichever way you turn this silver and turquoise box, it will always look the same.

Turning pinwheel
Whichever way you turn this pinwheel, it will always look the same. Pinwheels have rotational symmetry.

Rotational test
Trace over the four cats and girls and then cut your drawing along the dotted lines. If you cut patterns with rotational symmetry into equal halves or quarters, each part will be the same as the others.

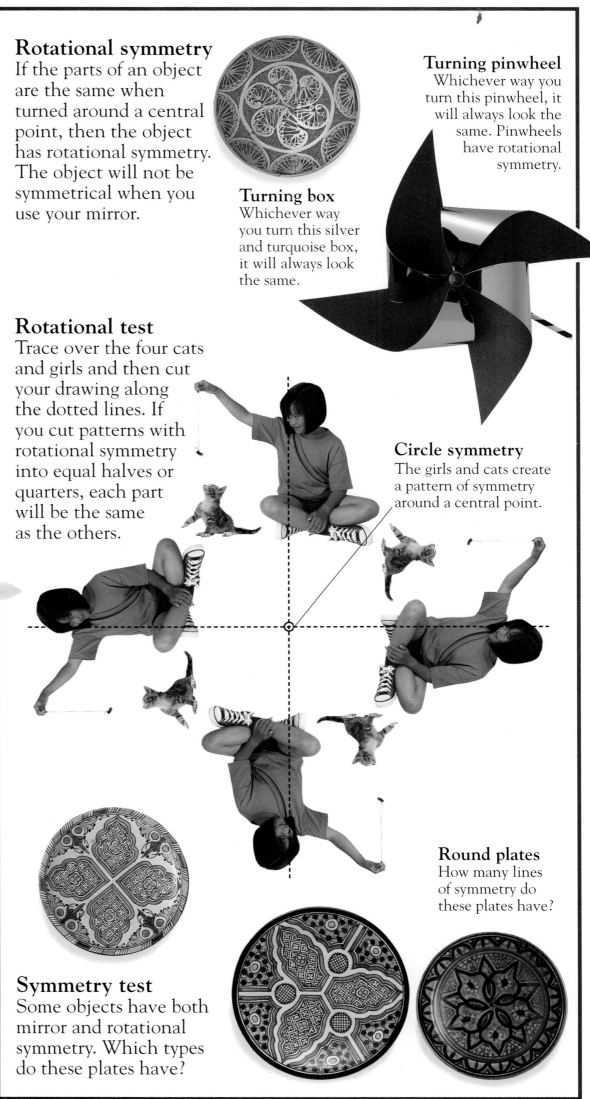

Circle symmetry
The girls and cats create a pattern of symmetry around a central point.

Round plates
How many lines of symmetry do these plates have?

Symmetry test
Some objects have both mirror and rotational symmetry. Which types do these plates have?

Stars and polygons

A polygon is a shape with many sides. In a regular polygon, all the sides are the same length and all the angles are the same. You can draw stars inside any regular polygon with more than four sides. Each polygon produces its own kind of star. You can also draw stars within stars.

Five-pointed stars in a pentagon
Follow these steps to draw stars inside a pentagon, a five-sided polygon.

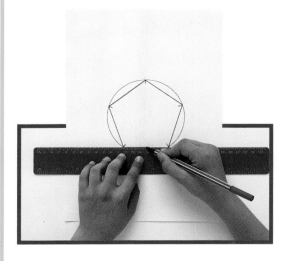

1 Mark the pentagon points using the symbols around the circle stencil on the flap. Join the points to draw the pentagon.

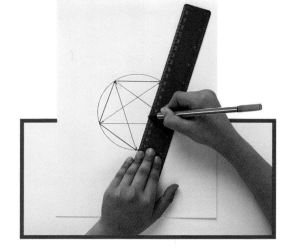

2 Rule a line to join every other corner on the pentagon. You will draw a star with five points.

Small pentagon
The middle of the star forms a small pentagon.

Star symmetry
Use your mirror bookmark to check the symmetry of your star.

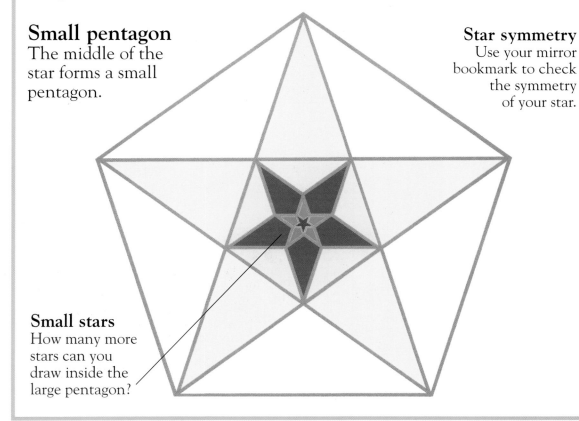

Small stars
How many more stars can you draw inside the large pentagon?

More stars within polygons
Use the circle stencil to draw a hexagon (a six-sided polygon) and an octagon (an eight-sided polygon). Try drawing stars inside these shapes.

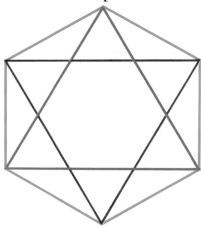

Six-pointed star in a hexagon
If you join every second corner inside a hexagon, you draw a triangle. What happens if you join the other corners?

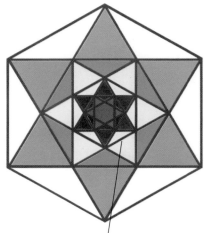

More small stars
Can you draw stars within stars inside a hexagon?

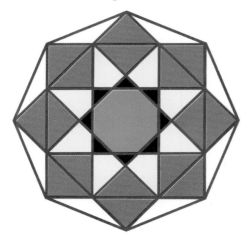

Eight-pointed star in an octagon
What shape do you draw if you join every second corner inside an octagon? What happens if you join every third corner?

Natural stars

How many kinds of stars can you find in nature?

Flower

How many points does this flower have?

How many points does the seed-case of an apple have?

Sand dollar

How many points does the star on a sand dollar have?

How many points does a starfish have?

Stars in a circle

You can draw many kinds of stars inside a circle that is divided into 12 equal parts. Use the circle stencil to draw five circles. Mark each one with 12 divisions like a clock and number them. When you draw your stars, always start at 12, at the top of the circle.

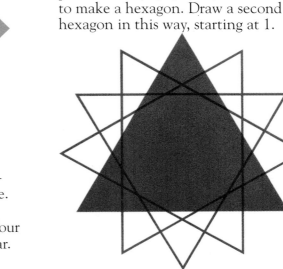

Star from hexagons

Rule lines to join every second point – 12, 2, 4, 6, 8, 10, and 12 – to make a hexagon. Draw a second hexagon in this way, starting at 1.

Star from squares

Rule lines to join every third point – 12, 3, 6, 9, and 12 – to make a square. Now join 1, 4, 7, 10, and 1 to make another square. Join the remaining four points on the circle to finish your star.

Twelve-pointed star

What happens when you join every fifth point on the edge of the circle – 12, 5, 10, 3, and so on?

Star from triangles

Join every fourth point – 12, 4, 8, and 12. What shape have you made? Now start at 1 and join every fourth point – 1, 5, 9, and 1. Do the same thing starting at 2, and then at 3. How many triangles make up this new star?

Lots of stars

Draw all four stars together in your last circle. Use a different colored marker for each star.

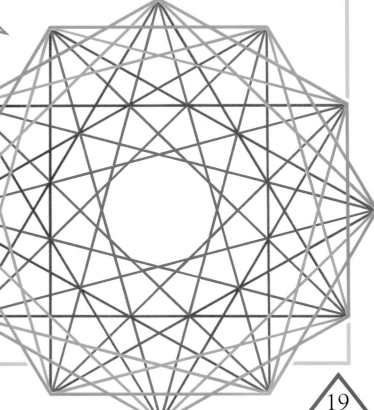

Patterns

Patterns are everywhere – on your clothes, on objects around your home, and outdoors. Most patterns are made up of an arrangement of a single type of object, a group of objects, or a sequence of shapes and colors.

A single object
You can repeat one type of object in different positions to make patterns.

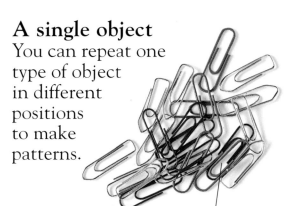

This is not a pattern
There is no order to how these paper clips have been scattered.

This is a pattern
These paper clips have been arranged into an orderly pattern.

A group of objects
You can use groups of objects to make patterns.

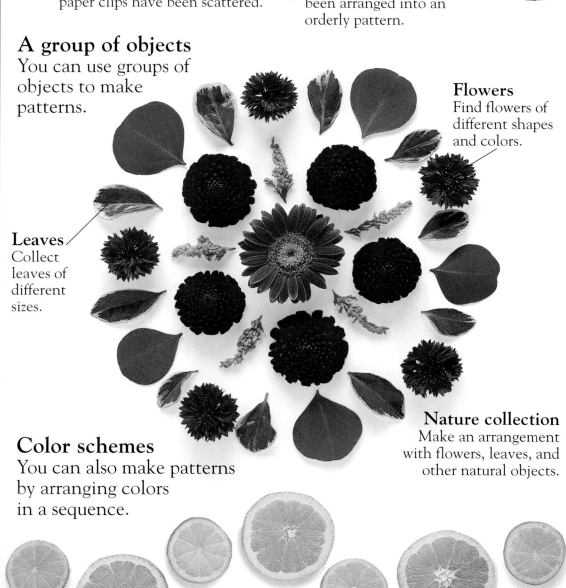

Flowers
Find flowers of different shapes and colors.

Leaves
Collect leaves of different sizes.

Nature collection
Make an arrangement with flowers, leaves, and other natural objects.

Color schemes
You can also make patterns by arranging colors in a sequence.

Animal patterns
The skins of many animals are covered with striking patterns.

Snake skin
The red stripes are a warning to other animals that this snake is poisonous.

Tiger stripes
A tiger has stripes to help it hide from prey in the light and shade under trees.

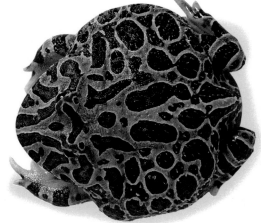

Horned toad
This toad has patterned skin to camouflage it on the forest floor.

Printing line patterns

Choose a simple shape, such as a figure seven, to make a line pattern. Try mixing the normal seven with a backward seven. How many patterns can you make out of lines of sevens? Can you find any lines of symmetry in your designs?

Row of sevens
A line of sevens, all facing the same direction

Upside down
Two pairs of sevens, each back-to-front and upside down

Touching sevens
The top sevens sit back-to-back, and the bottom sevens sit front-to-front and upside down.

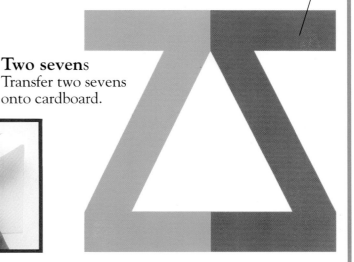

Two sevens
Transfer two sevens onto cardboard.

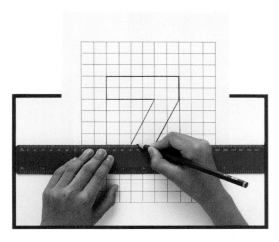

1 Draw a seven inside a square with sides made up of six small squares. Use the square grid at the back of this book to help you.

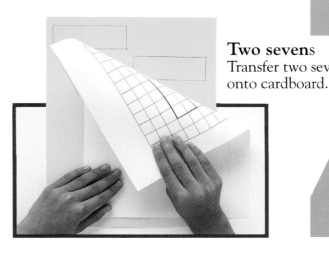

2 Turn the paper over and scribble on the back of the seven with pencil to smudge the seven's outline onto cardboard.

Back to front
Mount one shape like a normal seven and one like a backward seven.

3 Cut out the two sevens. Then mount them on more cardboard to make printing blocks.

4 Carefully brush some thick paint on both sevens. Use a different color for each block.

5 Press each block on paper, paint side down, to print.

Designing patterns

Printed patterns are designed using a basic shape called a motif, which is repeated in a grid to cover a surface. How many things around you are decorated with patterns?

Printing on paper
Print your own gift wrap and stationery using several motifs like the ones shown below.

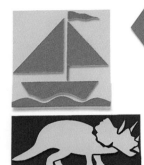

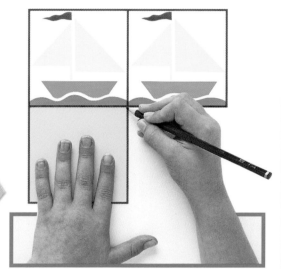

1 Make several blocks of cardboard in the shape of squares, diamonds, and rectangles. Design some motifs and glue them onto printing blocks.*

2 Make a print. Before you lift the block, trace around it with a pencil. For the next print, place the block next to the pencil line. Repeat this lots of times.

Erase the lines
Erase the pencil lines when you have covered the paper with your pattern.

Brick print
Can you copy this brick pattern with your rectangular printing block?

Designer collection
Put several designs onto printing blocks of the same shape and size. How many patterns can you create with your collection?

Diamond pattern
Use a diamond-shaped printing block to make patterns like this.

*There are full instructions for making printing blocks on page 21.

Abstract patterns
An abstract motif does not look like a real object or person, although you can base abstract motifs on real things.

Is it a bird?
Print with this abstract motif, based on a bird. What happens if you use different colors of paint and paper?

Dark on light
Try printing in a dark color on light paper.

Light on dark
Try printing in a light color on dark paper.

Traditional patterns

For thousands of years, people from all over the world have enjoyed decorating everyday things with patterns. Some patterns are abstract, while others are easy to recognize. Which of the patterns on this page do you think were inspired by nature?

Blanket
This blanket is woven with line patterns by the Navajo people of North America.

Patterned scarf
This scarf is patterned with a motif that looks like flowers and leaves.

Woven purse
The weave of this purse from Indonesia makes yellow, green, and purple squares.

Book cover
This diamond pattern is printed on the cover of a handmade book from Nepal.

Indian star
This star is decorated with lines of tiny sequins and glass shapes.

This ribbon is woven with a tartan pattern made of squares and stripes.

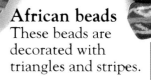

African beads
These beads are decorated with triangles and stripes.

Japanese bowl
This porcelain bowl is patterned with shapes like fish scales.

Soapstone egg
This egg is carved with overlapping shapes like feathers.

Mexican beads
These beads are painted with zigzag lines, triangles, and abstract shapes.

Indian purse
This embroidered purse is covered with beads and tiny mirrors sewn into shapes with thread.

This African bowl is woven of bright colors.

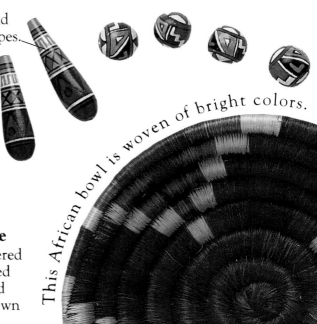

Double images

Some pictures seem to change depending on how you look at them. These pictures are called optical illusions and can seem to move around on the page or even trick your eyes into seeing something that isn't there.

Striped zebras

This drawing is made completely of stripes. Can you see two zebras?

Front or back

Which of these zebras appears to be in front?

Victor Vasarely Zebres 1944 © ADAGP Paris and DACS, London 1994

Strange shapes

Can you see two pictures in any of the drawings below?

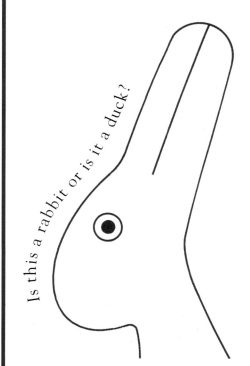

Is this a rabbit or is it a duck?

Yellow or white

Is there a difference in the shape of the yellow or the white parts of the pattern shown below?

Vase or faces

Do you see a vase, or do you see two faces looking at one another?

Fish and turtles

Fish and turtles cover the whole surface in this pattern. Can you see any spaces between the shapes?

Jumping patterns

Some patterns can seem to leap around in front of your eyes.

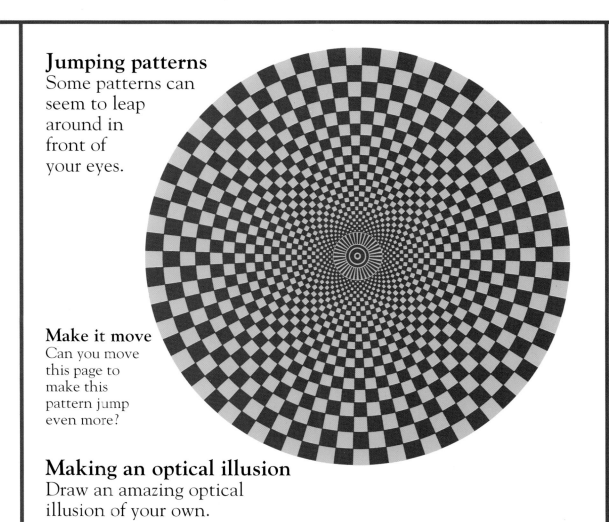

Make it move

Can you move this page to make this pattern jump even more?

Making an optical illusion

Draw an amazing optical illusion of your own.

1 Draw straight lines close together using a ruler and a thick felt pen or colored pencil.

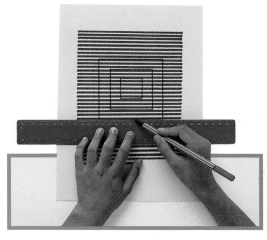

2 Draw a square with sides six grid squares long,* then draw two smaller squares inside it.

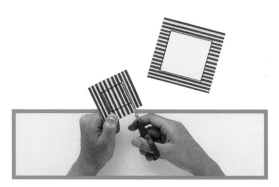

3 Carefully cut out the three striped squares. Discard the rest of the sheet of paper.

4 What happens if you turn the middle square at right angles to the other two squares?

Pictures from lines

You can make different effects by drawing pictures made up only of straight lines. Try leaving wide or thin spaces between the lines.

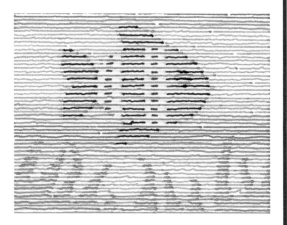

Between the lines

First draw the fish's outline, then fill it in with lines between the water lines.

Lines and spaces

Try using lines of different thicknesses and leave some space between them.

Stripes

Glue your striped squares to cardboard. Do the lines move?

Lines

What happens if you stripe the squares in black and white?

*Your square will be made up of 36 small squares.

Tessellating shapes

Polygons can be arranged to cover a surface without leaving any space between them. This type of pattern is called a tessellation. Tessellating polygons are often used as tiles for surfaces such as floors and walls.

Tessellating with one shape

Triangles, hexagons, and squares are the only regular polygons that can cover a surface completely. Regular polygons are shapes where all the sides are the same length and all the corner angles are the same.

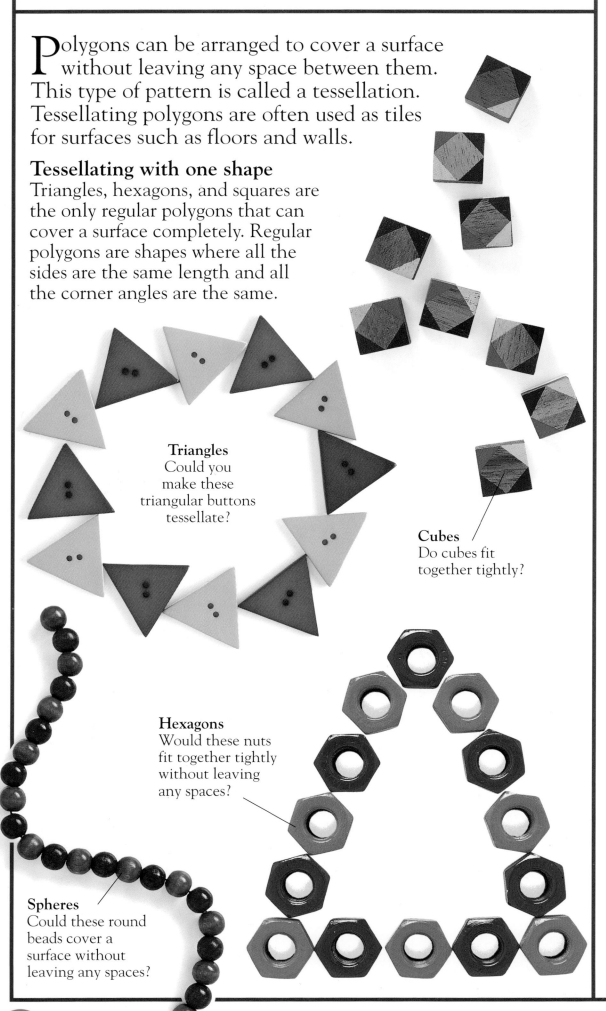

Triangles
Could you make these triangular buttons tessellate?

Cubes
Do cubes fit together tightly?

Hexagons
Would these nuts fit together tightly without leaving any spaces?

Spheres
Could these round beads cover a surface without leaving any spaces?

Patterns from polygons
Can you think of any objects that have regular polygons covering their whole surface?

Woven purse
Can you draw the shape that covers the surface of this woven purse from Indonesia?

Honeycomb
What shape forms the cells of a bee's honeycomb?

Puppet
What shape covers this puppet's dress?

Making tessellations
Practice covering a surface with combinations of shapes.

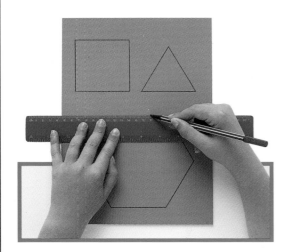

1 Use the stencils at the back of this book to draw a triangle, square, and hexagon on cardboard. All the shapes have sides of equal length. You may want to go over your pencil outlines with a marker and ruler.

2 Cut out the three shapes and trace around them onto colored paper. Cut out all the triangles, squares, and hexagons.

Shape challenge
Experiment with tessellating shapes to make patterns. Try using only squares and triangles, only triangles and hexagons, or try mixing all three shapes together.

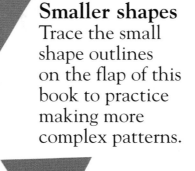

Smaller shapes
Trace the small shape outlines on the flap of this book to practice making more complex patterns.

Tile designs
Put together a combination of shapes as a tile design. Repeat your tile design to cover a surface. Try repeating the tile designs below. How many tiles can you design using hexagons, squares, and triangles?

Tile symmetry
Use your mirror to see if your designs have symmetry.

Tile style
You can create different effects by using shapes in contrasting colors.

Drawing tiles
Put some white paper over the triangular grid at the front of this book. Draw patterns over the grid lines, then make all or part of a pattern into a tile.

Patterns from grids

For thousands of years, people around the world have based patterns on simple grids, such as the square and triangular grids printed at the front and back of this book. Can you figure out which patterns on these two pages are based on each grid? Try drawing your own patterns using the grids.

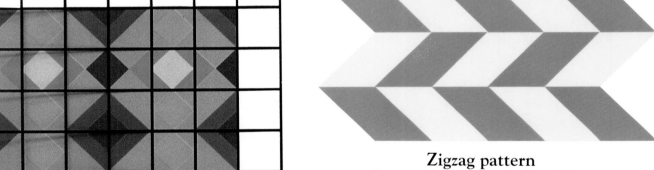

Star pattern
Can you draw this pattern? Which grid do you need?

Star
This shape can be made up of six diamonds or 12 triangles.

Hexagon
This shape can be made with six triangles.

Making a grid-tester
To check for the grid lines in the patterns on these two pages, first trace a section of each grid onto tracing paper, then hold your traces over each pattern.

Lines over lines
Place a grid-tester over the pattern. Which lines match up? You will soon see if the pattern was drawn on the square or the triangular grid.

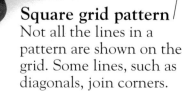

Zigzag pattern
Can you figure out which grid this zigzag pattern is based on?

Square grid pattern
Not all the lines in a pattern are shown on the grid. Some lines, such as diagonals, join corners.

Square pattern
This square pattern is made up of triangles. Which grid is it based on?

Petal pattern
Do you remember learning how to draw this pattern on page 13? Is it based on the triangular grid?

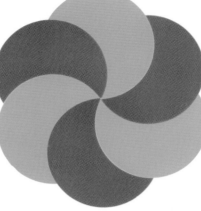

Swirly pattern
Which grid is this swirly pattern based on? Use your grid-tester to find out.

Octagonal pattern
Is this pattern based on the square or the triangular grid?

Circle pattern
Can you make a pattern of overlapping circles, like this? Use the circles printed on the square grid at the back of this book to help you.

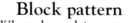

Block pattern
What does this pattern remind you of? Is it based on the square grid?

Rangoli designs
In Asia, doorsteps, paths, roads, and even people are decorated with traditional "rangoli" patterns in honor of a special event such as a wedding. These complicated patterns are often based on geometric grids.

Henna patterns
Asian artists paint rangoli patterns on hands and feet with special henna-dye, made from plants.

Green to brown
Henna leaves are ground into a green powder that is mixed with lemon juice to make a red–brown dye.

Secret signals
The initials of the bride and groom are often hidden in these patterns.

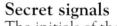

Tangrams and fractals

A tangram is an ancient Chinese puzzle with seven pieces that fit into a square. The object of the game is to make pictures using all seven pieces.

A fractal is a pattern where a basic motif is repeated again and again, each time getting smaller by the same amount. Fractals are often drawn on computers.

Making a tangram

You can make your own tangram game.

One quarter
This triangle is one quarter of the full square.

1 Trace this square, which is made up of all the tangram pieces.

One eighth
This square is one eighth of the full square.

One eighth
This triangle is one eighth of the full square.

Making pictures

Try making up your own tangram pictures.

2 Transfer the tangram square onto colored cardboard and cut out the pieces.

Tangram teaser

Can you make the bottom three tangram shapes? To help you, we have shown how three other shapes are made up.

woman

bird

sailboat

cat

duck

man

Fractals

The patterns on this page are called fractals. Can you see how the motif is repeated in each fractal?

Detailed pattern

Put some thin paper over the detailed grid printed in the special square on the square grid at the back of this book. Try drawing this pattern for yourself.

Computer fractal

A special computer program was needed to draw this beautiful and complicated fractal.

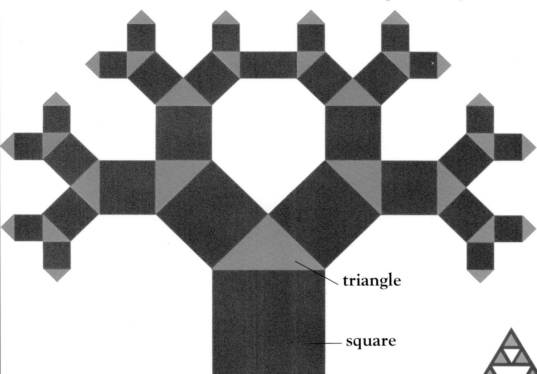

triangle

square

Tree fractal

This fractal grows outward like a tree. The repeated motif looks like a house – a square with a triangle roof. The long side of each triangle is the same as the side of the square it joins on to.

Triangle fractal

This fractal starts with one large triangle divided into four smaller triangles. The pattern grows inside the outer three triangles in each group. Try drawing this fractal using the more detailed grid printed in the special triangle area on the triangular grid.

Reverse triangles

Now try coloring in the middle triangle of each group, leaving the other triangles white. Do you get a different effect?

Large and small

Look closely at the fractal patterns on this page. Can you see how the smallest part of each pattern is like the largest part of the fractal?

Middle triangle

The triangle in the middle of each group is left white. The other triangles in each group are colored green.

Solid shapes

Some arrangements of flat shapes can be made into three-dimensional (3-D) solid shapes. Try making up these solid shapes from patterns of squares and triangles, all with sides of equal length.

Making a cube

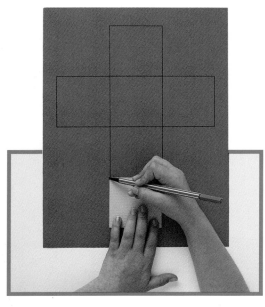

1 Use the square stencil at the back of this book to make a square template. Draw around the template six times on cardboard to make the cube pattern shown on the right. Add tabs for gluing.

2 Cut around the outer edges of the squares and tabs. Run a ballpoint pen tip along the edge of a ruler to score along all the lines.

3 Decorate the same side of the cardboard as the side you have just scored, then bend along the score lines. Glue the tabs and finish making up the cube.

Finished cube
Keep one side of the cube open as a lid. You can use the cube to keep things in, or as a gift box.

Patterns for solid shapes
Use these flat patterns to make two 3-D solid shapes.

Cube pattern

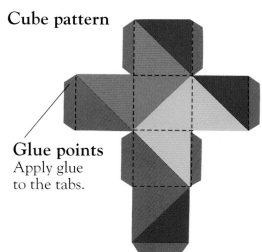

Glue points
Apply glue to the tabs.

Tetrahedron pattern

Triangles
Decorate the four triangles with smaller triangles.

Making a tetrahedron
Use the triangle stencil to make a triangle template and then draw four triangles in the pattern above on cardboard. Follow the instructions for making up the cube to make up a tetrahedron.

Sides of a tetrahedron
How many sides does a tetrahedron have?

More patterns and volumes

You can make some larger solid shapes by using more triangles or by combining triangles with squares. Copy the patterns below and make some amazing 3-D shapes.

Octahedron pattern

Icosahedron pattern

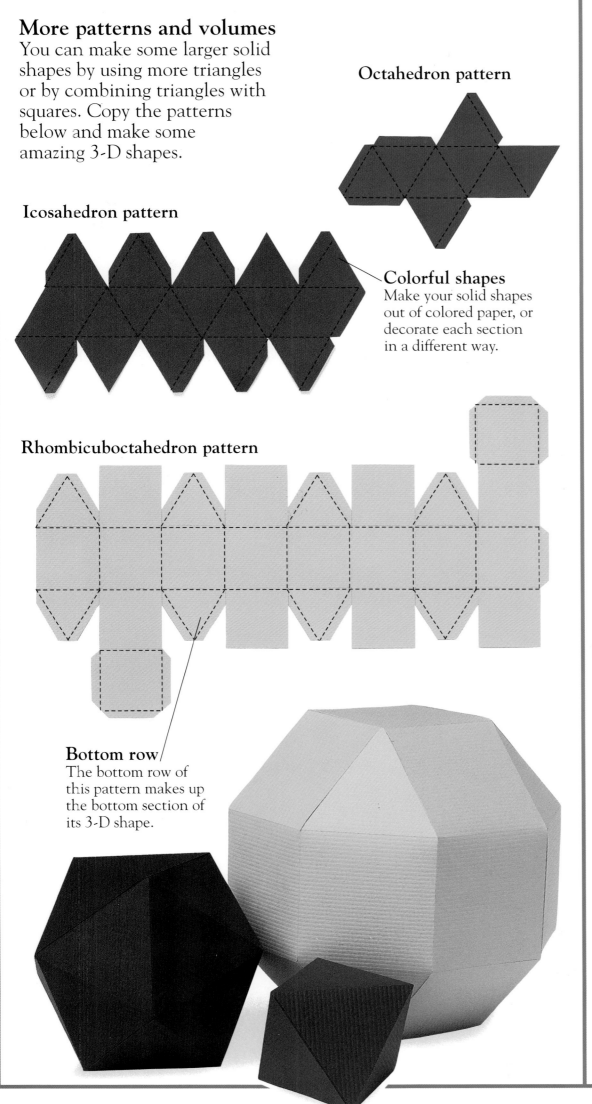

Colorful shapes

Make your solid shapes out of colored paper, or decorate each section in a different way.

Rhombicuboctahedron pattern

Bottom row

The bottom row of this pattern makes up the bottom section of its 3-D shape.

Open shapes

Can you make these open 3-D shapes out of straws and balls of modeling clay? Which model holds its shape the best?

Open tetrahedron

A tetrahedron has three triangles on a triangle base.

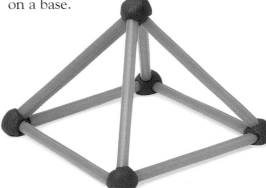

Open pyramid

A pyramid has four triangles on a base.

Open cube

A cube is made up of six equal squares.

33

Pattern puzzles

Test your memory with the games and puzzles on these two pages. How much have you remembered from doing the activities in this book? If you're not sure of an answer, look back through the book to help you figure it out.

How many circles can you find on these two pages?

Starfish
In which polygon could you draw a five-pointed star like this starfish?

Patterned peacock
What shape is repeated in this peacock's tail?

Secret shape
What shape can you make up from these eight parts?

Bunches of flowers
Use your mirror to make this girl hold her flowers up in the air, or close to her chest.

Can you find the center of this shell?

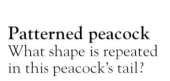

Chinese puzzle
Can you make these seven pieces into a woman?

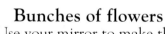

How many shapes can you find in this picnic meal?

Woven shapes
What shapes have been
woven into this bag from Java?

Tile test
Can you find the repeat
in the pattern on this tile?

Patterned jug
Can you find the
repeats in the line
patterns on this jug?

Does this sunflower have mirror symmetry?

Flower
Does this lily have
rotational symmetry?

Triangle teaser
What polygon can you make with
these triangles?

How many triangles can you find on these two pages?

Tile flower
What shape can
you see in the center
of this flower pattern
made from Moroccan tiles?

Patterned clothes
How many different
patterns can you
see on the clothes
of these children?

Yellow and white
Is there a difference
between the yellow
and white parts of
this pattern?

Words about shapes

abstract
Abstract shapes and patterns do not look exactly like any real thing.
pages 22, 23

angle
An angle is the space in a corner where two lines meet.
pages 18, 26

circle
A circle is a round 2-D shape.
pages 10, 12, 13, 14, 18, 19, 26, 29

cone
A cone is a 3-D shape that narrows from a circle to a point.
pages 10, 11

crescent
A crescent is part of a circle, in the shape of a quarter moon.
page 10

cube
A cube is a 3-D shape made up of six equal squares.
pages 10, 11, 14, 26, 32, 33

cuboid
A cuboid is a 3-D shape with an equal square at each end, and four equal rectangles in between.
page 10

cylinder
A cylinder is a 3-D shape with an equal circle at each end and one curved surface.
pages 10, 11

design
A design is a plan that shows how to make something. To design is to create such a plan.
pages 21, 27

diagonal line
A diagonal line joins two corners of a shape.
page 13

diamond
A diamond is a 2-D shape with two sets of equal sides and equal angles in its opposite corners.
pages 10, 14, 22

fractal
A fractal is a pattern made up of a repeated motif that gets smaller by the same amount with each repetition.
pages 30, 31

grid
A grid is a regular arrangement of lines on which patterns can be based.
pages 21, 22, 25, 28–31

heart
A heart is a 2-D shape with two half circles at the top and a point at the bottom.
page 10

hexagon
A hexagon is a 2-D shape with six equal sides and equal angles in its corners.
pages 10, 11, 14, 18, 19, 26, 27

icosahedron
An icosahedron is a 3-D shape made up of 20 regular triangles.
page 33

kirigami
Kirigami is the Japanese art of making patterns by folding and cutting paper.
page 15

line of symmetry
A line of symmetry is the line that divides an object into two halves that are the same.
pages 16, 17

mirror symmetry
A design has mirror symmetry, or reflective symmetry, when the part that is reflected in a mirror is the same as the part hidden behind the mirror.
pages 16–18, 21, 27

motif
A motif is a group of shapes that is repeated to make a pattern.
pages 22, 23

octagon
An octagon is a 2-D shape with eight equal sides and equal angles.
pages 18, 29

octahedron
An octahedron is a 3-D shape made up of eight regular triangles.
page 33

optical illusion
An optical illusion is a pattern or drawing that tricks the eye.
pages 24, 25

oval

An oval is a 2-D shape like a stretched circle. It is longer from end to end than across the middle.
page 10

pattern

A pattern is made up of a motif that is repeated.
pages 17, 20–25

pentagon

A pentagon is a 2-D shape with five equal sides and equal angles.
pages 10, 18

polygon

A polygon is a shape with many sides. In a regular polygon, all the sides are the same length and all the angles of the corners are the same.
pages 18, 26

pyramid

A pyramid is a 3-D shape made up of four triangles on a base.
pages 10, 33

rectangle

A rectangle is a 2-D shape with four sides, of which two opposite sides are longer than the other two sides.
pages 10, 12, 15, 22

rhombicuboctahedron

A rhombicuboctahedron is a 3-D shape made up of 18 squares and eight regular triangles.
page 33

rotational symmetry

If an object or pattern can be turned around a central point and still look the same, it has rotational symmetry.
pages 16, 17

solid shape

A solid shape has height, width, and depth.
pages 10, 32

sphere

A sphere is a round 3-D shape.
pages 10, 26

square

A square is a 2-D shape with four equal sides and angles.
pages 10, 12, 14, 15, 19, 22, 26, 27, 30–33

star

A star is a 2-D shape with four or more points.
pages 10, 11, 18, 19, 28

tangram

A tangram is a Chinese puzzle in which pictures are made up from seven parts of a square.
page 30

tessellate

To tessellate is to cover a surface with polygons without leaving any space between them.
pages 26, 27

tetrahedron

A tetrahedron is a 3-D shape made up of four regular triangles.
pages 10, 32, 33

three-dimensional shape

A three-dimensional (3-D) shape has height, width, and depth.
pages 10, 32, 33

tile

A tile is a tessellating shape that is made up of one or more polygons.
pages 11, 26, 27

triangle

A triangle is a 2-D shape with three sides. A regular triangle has three equal sides and equal angles in its corners.
pages 10–12, 14, 15, 18, 19, 26, 27, 30–33

two-dimensional shape

A two-dimensional (2-D) shape is flat. It has only height and width.
pages 10, 32

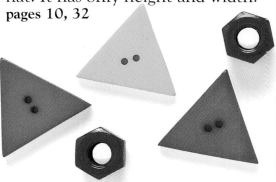

ACKNOWLEDGMENTS

Dorling Kindersley would like to thank the following for their help:

Picture credit
31tr Gregory Sams/Science Photo Library

Additional illustrations
Sally Kindberg; Coral Mula

Additional photography
Geoff Brightling; Jane Burton; Peter Chadwick; Andy Crawford; Geoff Dann; Andreas von Einsiedel; Peter Hayman; Colin Keates; Dave King; Cyril Laubscher; Stephen Oliver; Jerry Young

Models
Monica Byles; Ricci Clemente; Ebru Djemal; Josey Edwards; Richard Lygo; Julian Morris; Kelly Simpson; Jeremy Smith; Rosalyn Sullivan

Additional acknowledgments
Anju and Mrs. Puri at Shahnaz Herbal, 5A Bathurst Street, London W2 (Tel. 071 – 724 0440); Pietro at The Coffee Gallery, 23 Museum Street, London WC1 (Tel. 071 – 436 0455); Sarah Ashun; Mark Bracey; Karen Fielding; Jamie Lamshed; Lucy Pringle; Jenny Rayner; Silpa Shah

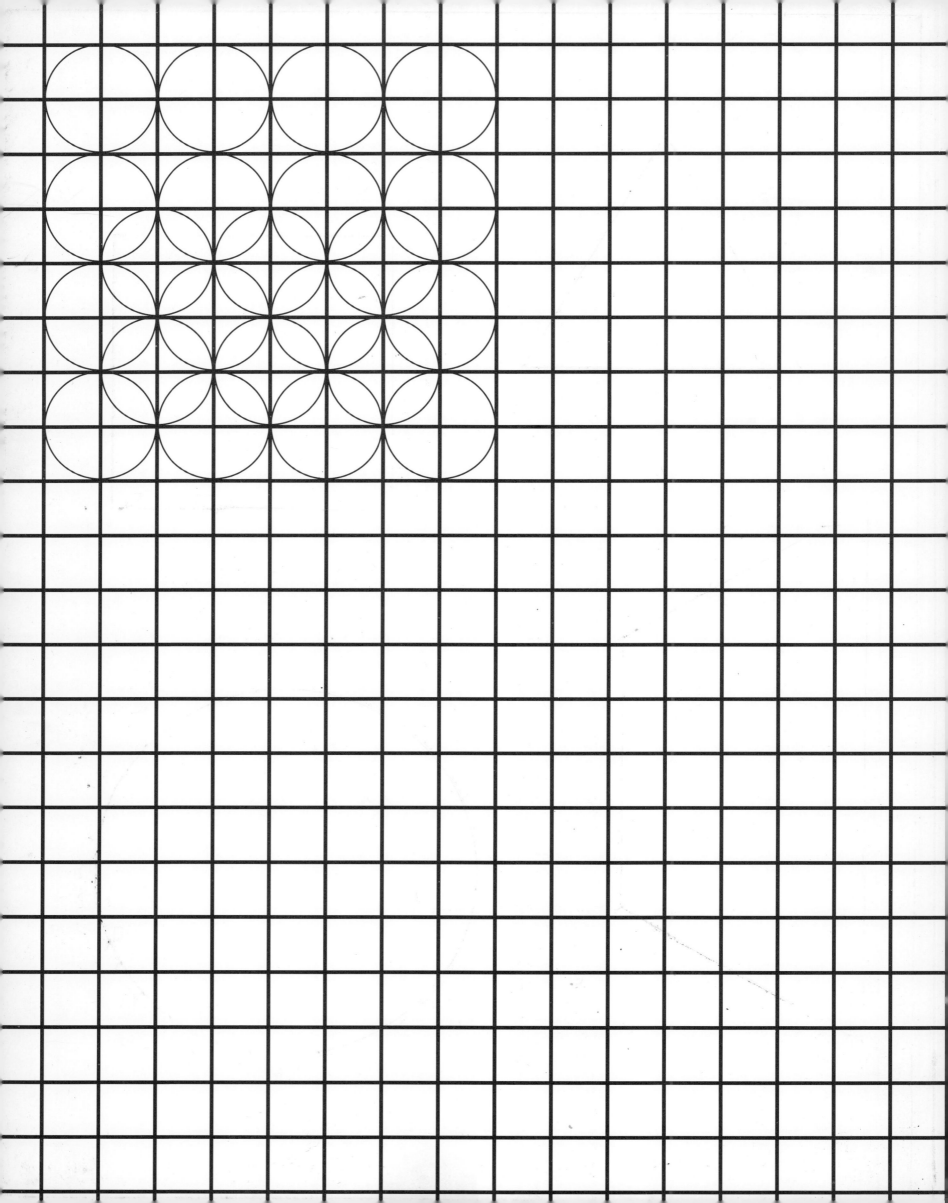